# A WADD

# PENGUINS

and other fun
collective nouns

Little Lion Publishing UK

Written by Stephanie Lipsey-Liu
Illustrated by Jemma Dando

For Isabella and Toby

First printed 2021

ISBN 978-1-7399336-1-6
Little Lion Publishing UK
Nottingham, England
www.facebook.com/littlelionpublishing

This Little Lion book
belongs to

••••••••••••••••••••••••••••••••••••••••••••

Stick together and keep warm!
It's a waddle of penguins!

Penguins have their own individual voices just like people.

This helps them find their mates in a big waddle of penguins.

Did you know?

Once penguins are in the water we call them a raft of penguins.

A waddle is only when they're on land.

Did you know penguins can't fly?
However, they are excellent swimmers!
When they are hunting for fish in the sea,
they swallow a lot of sea water.
Luckily they can sneeze it out again! Achoo!

Look out! Shaaaaaaark!
Five sharks!
Argh, it's a whole shiver of sharks!

4

Did you know?

Sharks are the only type of fish that have eyelids.

Sharks give birth to baby sharks instead of laying eggs like most fish.
Baby sharks are called pups!

Most sharks are cold-blooded which means their body temperature is the same as the water they swim in.

Ooo! Ouch! Watch out for that smack of jellyfish! They might sting you!

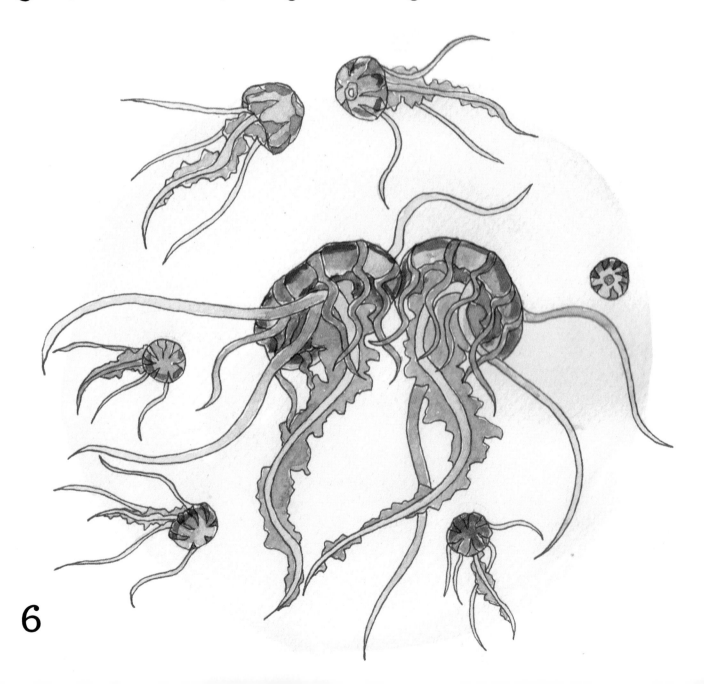

Jellyfish have been around for over 600 million years! That's before dinosaurs, before trees and even before fungi. Some jellyfish are actually immortal which means they can live forever.

Did you know?

Jellyfish don't have a brain, a heart or lungs.

Can you remember the name for a group of penguins on land? What about in water? Turn to pages 2 and 3 to see if you were right!

Between 2 and 30 dolphins is called a pod.
1000 dolphins make a superpod!
Can you imagine 1000 dolphins swimming together?

Dolphins are mammals, not fish. They breathe air through a blowhole on top of their heads. This means they need to come to the surface for air and cannot breathe underwater.

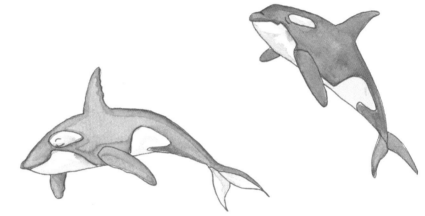

Did you know?

A killer whale, also known as an orca, is actually a type of dolphin? It's the biggest member of the dolphin family.

Can you remember the name for a group of sharks? Turn to page 4 to see if you were right!

Attention! Salute!
Double time, go go go!

A squadron of pelicans.

Both male and female pelicans help with building their nests, as well as taking it in turns to stand (not sit!) on the eggs until they hatch.

Did you know?

Pelicans use their huge bills to capture food but they don't store it there for long. They tip out the water then swallow their catch whole.

Can you remember the name for a group of jellyfish? Turn to page 6 to see if you were right.

What a sweet little family of otters. In fact, a group of otters doesn't have to be related to each other to be referred to as a family. That's actually the proper name for a group of otters.

Like penguins, when otters are in the water we say a raft of otters, instead of a family of otters.

Otters use rocks to crack open the shells of the clams they eat. They carry the rocks in loose skin pouches under their armpits!

Did you know?

Otters eat up to a quarter of their weight in food every single day!

Can you remember the name for a group of dolphins?
Turn to page 8 to see if you were right!

Caaaaan yooooouuuuu speeeeeeeak whaaaaaaaale? The collective noun for whales is a mob!

Bowhead whales can live for up to 200 years! This is probably because they live in such cold water.

Did you know?

Whales are the biggest animal to have ever lived on the planet, even bigger than dinosaurs. They are also the loudest animal and eat up to 40 million krill a day!

Can you remember the name for a group of pelicans? Turn to page 10 to see if you were right!

What do we have here? Not a mob, this time we have a bob of seals.

Seals in a group can also be called a colony, a rookery, a herd or a harem.

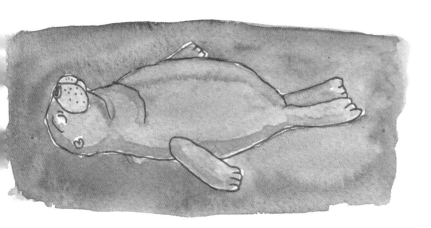

The female seal is called a cow, the male seal is called a bull and baby seals are called pups.

Did you know?

Seals can sleep underwater and hold their breath for up to 2 hours!

Can you remember the name for a group of otters? Turn to page 12 to see if you were right!

Look at all the beautiful fish! As they are all the same type of fish, we call them a school of fish.

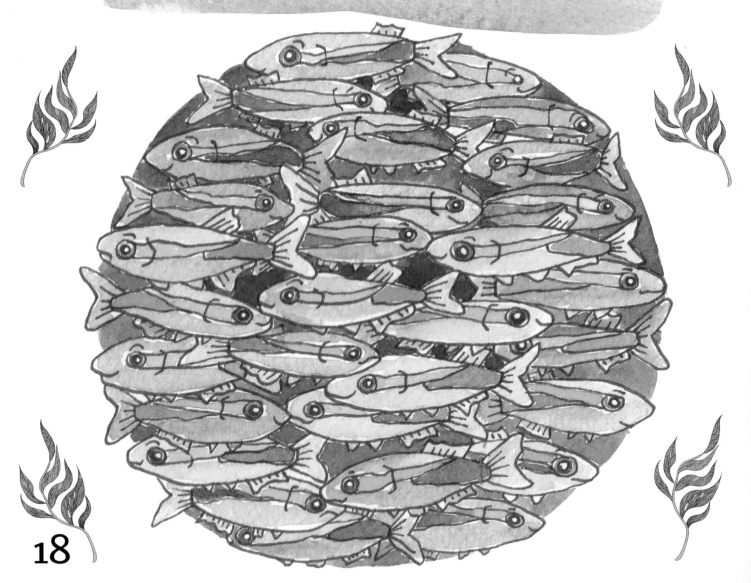

Did you know?

Neither starfish nor jellyfish are actually fish!

A shoal of fishes or a school of fish?
We say a shoal of fishes when there are lots of different types of fish in the group.
If they are all the same, then it's a school of fish.

Can you remember the name for a group of whales?
Turn to page 14 to see if you were right!

QUACK quack, quack quack, a paddling of ducks. Can you quack like a duck?

Ducks don't have any nerves or blood vessels in their feet so they can't feel the cold!

Did you know?

Ducks can see very well underwater. They can also see in more colours than humans and can see almost all the way around without turning their heads!

Can you remember the name for a group of seals? Turn to page 16 to see if you were right!

Can you juggle? What about do a somersault or breathe fire? I don't think a puffin can do any of these things, but we still call them a "circus of puffins".

Puffins are sometimes called "clowns of the sea". This is probably where their collective noun, "a circus of puffins" comes from.

Puffins can flap their wings up to 400 times in one minute. This is so fast that their wings will look like a blur.

Did you know?

Puffins love to live together. The largest circus of puffins had 4 million puffins in it!

Can you remember two names for a group of fish?
Turn to pages 18 and 19 to see if you were right!

A group of walruses can be called a huddle, a flock, a pod, a herd or an ugly of walruses. Whoever came up with the last one is a bit mean!

What eats a walrus? Only polar bears and orcas!

A huddle of walruses is usually made up of all females or all males. All walruses have huge tusks which help them to get out of the sea!

All animals have a scientific name which is in an old language called Latin. The walrus's name translates to "tooth-walking-sea-horse"!

Can you remember the name for a group of ducks? Turn to page 20 to see if you were right!

# Glossary

**Collective:**
People, animals or things that can be grouped together as a whole.

**Digestion:**
The breakdown of food so it can be used by the body.

**Krill:**
A small crustacean similar to shrimp which are eaten by many sea animals.

**Mob:**
A large crowd of people that want to cause trouble or violence.

Nerves:
Bundles of fibres in the body that send information to and from the brain. Nerves are how we feel things like temperature and pain.

Raft:
Materials that float such as wood, tied together to make a floating platform.

Shiver:
When your body shakes slightly, very quickly because it is cold.

Squadron:
A group of people in the Army, Navy or Royal Air Force.

## About the Author

Stephanie was born on the Wirral and now lives in Nottingham with her husband, daughter, pack of dogs, shoal of fishes and a mischief of rats. She is an optician but when she is not testing eyes she can be found sewing, playing the piano, practising sign language, singing and/or adventuring with her family.

## About the Illustrator

Jemma was born in Wiltshire in England but now lives in Cardiff in Wales with her fiancée and pounce of cats. When she's not drawing or teaching her lovely little learners, she can be found campervanning, kayaking and climbing mountains.

28

# Fill in the blanks!!

A _____ of penguins.

A _____ of sharks.

A _____ of jellyfish.

A _____ of dolphins.

A _____ of pelicans.

A _____ of otters.

A _____ of whales.

A ____ of seals.

A _____ of fishes.

A _____ of ducks.

A _____ of puffins.

An _____ of walrus.

Can you remember the name for a group of puffins and a group of walruses? Turn to page 22 and 24 to see if you were right!

If you enjoyed A Waddle of Penguins, look out for our next collective noun book, A Mischief of Elves! The first book in the series, A Fluffle of Bunnies is out now!

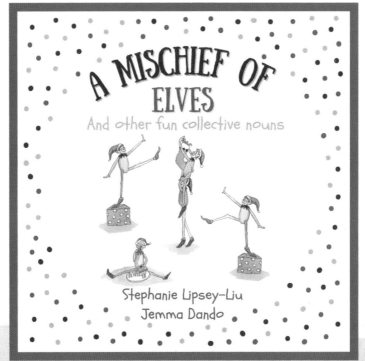

We would LOVE it if you could leave us a review on Amazon! Get your adult to help you with what to write. If you would like to share a picture of you reading A Waddle of Penguins, please tag us on Facebook @littlelionpublishinguk or on Instagram @littlelionpublishing.